The poems of *Rivers in Your Skin, Sirens in Your Hair* transport us from "dream to magic to grotesquerie" with exquisite attentiveness. Whether exploring the barnacled, psychological depths of "the Unlocking Room" or tracking the transformation of Rapunzel's hair into light-seeking fungi, Pichette's poems are steeped in the rich cross-pollination of the mythic and environmental. A luminous debut.

—Katherine Larson, award-winning author of *Radial Symmetry*.

Every one of Marisca's poems is imbued with a wild fairytale magic: sometimes dark, others whimsical, but never once failing to grab you by the heartstrings. In this miraculous book of speculative poetry, moths dance with moss and memories, while sirens sing seaweed-tangled tales that will linger past the last poem.

—Avra Margariti, author of *Saint of Witches*

Pichette's *River in Your Skin, Sirens in Your Hair* has the lyrical timelessness of whale songs; it is the effortless drift and gentle, yet striking, beauty of jellyfish; the heartrending notes of a ballad; the curtain-drop upon the conclusion of a tragedy, with the passionate applause still ringing in our ears and the sharp pain of our palms lingering, itching; and it is a walk down a desolate, dimly lit street, with a dying candle held between our hands."

—Ai Jiang, author of *Linghun*.

Simultaneously mythic and intimate, *Rivers in Your Skin, Sirens in Your Hair* initiates you into a world of mycelial princesses and glass slipper urns, as delicate as it is sinister, as grotesque as it is full of grace. The waters of Marisca Pichette's debut are pearl-encrusted, dark with seaweed, host to a whole ecosystem of mysterious denizens. The reward for plunging in is mouthwatering language, irresistible rhythm, and that deep full-bodied chill that all good poetry blooms in us.

—Sienna Tristen, author of *The Heretic's Guide to Homecoming* and *hortus animarum: a new herbal for the queer heart*

RIVERS IN YOUR SKIN, SIRENS IN YOUR HAIR

RIVERS IN YOUR SKIN, SIRENS IN YOUR HAIR

Poems

MARISCA PICHETTE

Android Press

PERMISSIONS

"These days were made for us" — original publication: *Mass Poetry* (2018)

"She gathered up the dust" — original publication: *Frozen Wavelets* (2023)

"Kitchen Garden" — original publication: *Savant-Garde* (2022)

"What roots she has her own" — original publication: *Kaleidotrope* (2022)

"I never learned the word" — original publication: Blue Unicorn (2022)

"In the Unlocking Room" — original publication: *Eye to the Telescope* (2022)

"Where We Felt With Moss" — original publication: *On Spec* (2022)

"Nobyl" — original publication: *Solarpunk Magazine* (2022)

"For a place in the family of things" — original publication: *Channel Magazine* (2020)

"charybdis" — original publication: *The Future Fire* (2022)

"What do you remember about the earth?" — original publication: In this Together Exhibition (2021)

"While Alice sleeps in Wonderland" — original publication:

Apparition Lit (2022)

"In the middle" — original publication: *Eye to the Telescope* (2022)

"At the Wedding of Death and Time" — original publication: *Enchanted Living* (2021)

"The Ossuary at Ocean's End" — original publication: *Mermaids Monthly* (2021)

"Aequinoctium" — original publication: *Ghost Orchid Press* (2021)

"Killing whale" — original publication: *Ligeia Magazine* (2022)

"Victor II" — original publication: *Snow-Capped Press* (2021)

"Topsoil" — original publication: *Solarpunk Magazine* (2022)

"And it dries and dries" — original publication: *Haven Spec* (2022)

"Mary Celeste" — original publication: *Zeniada Magazine* (2018)

"Oddkin" — original publication: *Seaside Gothic* (2022)

"and" — original publication: *Black Cat Magazine* (2021)

"Heel to Toe" — original publication: *BSFS Honorable Mention* (2022)

"The Art of Betraying Others for Food" — original publication: *Coffin Bell* (2022)

"the glaciers made her deep" — original publication: *Gwyllion Magazine* (2021)

"Wait when ice forms over my fingertips" — original publication: *Of Horror and Hope* (2022)

"Syph" — original publication: *Star*Line* (2022)

"Coronation" — original publication: *Star*Line* (2022)
"Seeing-holes" — original publication: *Star*Line* (2022)

For those whom the stories never fit.

CONTENTS

INTRODUCTION

In poetry, I never claimed to know what I was doing. I still struggle to call myself A Poet. As a prose writer, I didn't learn poetic forms or terms for rhythm and conceit. I apologize.

That said, these poems are born from the same place where all creative work grows. They come from a desire to tell a new story, or an old story in a new way. They embody a search for freedom from constraint, a space for authenticity.

I know what some of us are thinking. Isn't speculative poetry *inauthentic*? It tells a story outside of reality, after all.

Ah. But that makes it all the more authentic. By leaving reality behind, we access the rawest truths about ourselves.

From dream to magic to grotesquerie, I offer these poems to you. I hope you see in them a glimmer of memory, an echo of home.

Part One: rivers

In parting

When I left home I took only what I could carry:

seaglass, postcards, embroidery
thread woven between my fingers
circling my wrists.

I braided my hair with eggshells
& apple seeds, trussed together
under a paisley pashmina.

I wove pockets I'd accumulated:
stitches over my shoulders,
knees to accommodate Polaroids,
owl pellets, wax seals & vintage
stamps;

pillowcases bulging with stuffed
animals & clementines for later,
headphones for the bus, extra
USB cables wrapped around
My mother's perfume.

A doll, felted from my first cat's
fur. The jawbone of an English sheep.

With the Larousse, my pockets filled.
I turned to my collarbones, wedging
Playdough, fish food, pine needles
& glass beads into leftover spaces.

When I could carry no more—
my throat lined with academic papers
& diary entries rolled up in
rubber bands
—I stepped towards the door.

I forgot nothing as I left.

My last act: unscrewed bookshelves,
carefully folded
into the creases
of my skin.

These days were made for us

so tell me that rain
wasn't made for me

tell me that there's a difference
between diamonds and teardrops;

so tell me that seagulls
fear the ocean

tell them that water
isn't touchable, not really

—we all shrink away from things
that are bigger than us—

so tell the field that mud
is just shy soil

and that a hole is a memory
of bravery,

exploration and dirty shoes
that don't quite know the way.

so tell me that mud wasn't made
to remember where I go

and tell me that you fear the ocean
just like an eye fears a tear

and the clouds
fear the rain.

the size of your fist

I tried molding my heart—
carving it of golem clay
& incising my wish on its malleable skin:
love me back.

I fired it too long
& brittle, it broke
the day my ribs collapsed.

I decided metal was stronger
& forged my heart again
in the same mold.

Iron was too heavy
steel too cold
copper too weak
& green too soon.

Aluminum bent out of shape
just with words.
Metal, I realized,
is weakest of all.

I blew my heart of glass
decorated with chips
from all it was
before.

But I couldn't feel through my gloves
& I dropped that heart
before it ever had a chance
to beat.

Between the shards I saw
what had lain
underneath it
all this time.

I walked outside & found
an oak tree
broken by the storm.

From her fallenness I carved
heartwood dense
dark
sap dripping blood life
on my feet.

It took me three weeks
to whittle my heart.

Light, tough
smoother than glass
& warmer
than steel.

I placed my oaken heart
between bruised ribs
& folded closed my skin,
muscle knitting like bark.

On the first day
of the fourth week
my heart beat at last
its first pulse.

like breathing

a kind stranger once said
"rain is in the air."
water pools in my lungs,
lightning restarting my pulse,
thunder rumbling where my gut
should be.

I asked them under storm clouds
"will we drown?"
rain falls
wipes washes wrings my wrinkles
away.

all the years I worked for,
experience wearily won
absorbed by grass already dead
& the black holes of gutters.

they said between flashes
"we drink the years
like fine wine."
& in the arms of a jagged bolt
I lost them.

I swim home
paddling past strangers
kind & unkind
stranger & strange
swallowing thunder I wonder

about the kindness of strangers—
the strangeness of kindness—
the kind of strange
only stranger than kind.

my home is washed clean
by the storm.
I backstroke up the steps
& find myself in a living room
of fish.

drifting in their midst I ask them
if they have finally drunk
enough.

Her ribs are
apple wood

Her fingers long ago lost
their feeling.

Nails browning, abscising in
a breath lost

between her toes,
She colds & colds the winter

slumbering nailless, hairless,
skin chapped peeling into strips.

Where her children planted
grapevines wrap clothes to out

their colding. She colds
still in spring, her skin senescing

Flesh bared to the bees,
colorless arms too thin too dead

too little for homes to make.
A hole in her heart

invites them in, & colding
empty, filling motion she flies

& breathes
& buzzes

with them.

She gathered up
the dust

of herself
and could not find the glue.

So, despairing of a place
she took a breath, and blew—

The pieces fluttered from her hands
and sparkled, as they flew

to land at last
upon her past;

A house she never knew.

Kitchen Garden

in chalk you drew a line
between the Wilderness
and our childhood
spent in gardens we thought
were wild, walls we imagined
endured for centuries
and food we saw
in miracles.

your chalk was pink and orange
and sunset, summer days
washed back by spring
snow melt in your eyes when you said
you were leaving, when you said
so was i.

ivy and weeds force their way between my toes
occupy the palm you used to hold
as we went running through labyrinths
we pretended not to see in progress,
shears nipped out of memories

like tags removed from clothes.

you always swore we'd come back;
you always said you can't go back
can't replace the Wilderness spreading over the hills
into the vast horizon dripping in stories
with a plain old kitchen garden
as practical as our futures.

i'm sorry to say i didn't listen—not then
and not now as i leave the car running
door ajar, coat half-buttoned
shuffling through the broken gate
between ruined beds and gravel spread
like fish scales on the grass.

it really is a kitchen garden, neat (or was)
with onions, parsnips, chives and herbs
that flutter faint on the breeze.
half dry, half dead, half naturalized
wandering out into
a different kind of wilderness.

without you here, i fall into a squat
squint my eyes
clench my fists
and through blurred vision,
remember how our horizon
never ran out of sun.

What roots she has
her own

In the forgotten tower
she reads a library

forgotten worlds in
forgotten pages like and

nothing like her own.
Her forgotten room is small,

lined with shelves she reads
twelve hundred worlds together

holding her place with endless
strands of wheat-gold hair.

Sitting in her web of forgetting
she tugs, ties, binds

her forgotten present
to a thousand futures

unbraiding.

I never learned
the word

for drowned.

Watching ice crack
and crumble,
watching is not
a choice.

My thoughts

graze

Ursus major meandering over
a waning sky, chased
season after season

by the notion
of watching.

In the Unlocking Room

the doors are all round. Arches spread themselves
in marble and birch bark, caressing doors set deep
under their keystones.

Some keystones are marked. (I have marked them.)
A rotary dial in chalk over the door that leads
to my childhood; two crystal ornaments
flashing rainbows onto the door to summer;
a smear of dirt against the birch bark keystone
which holds the Beginning.

In the Unlocking Room I count my steps,
pacing its edges—really, there are no edges,
just the doors and their eventual openings—
round and round I go, slowing when I hear
Voices.

I talk frequently in the Unlocking Room. To myself
and to the doors, their keystones, the ceiling
(which is not a ceiling, but an observatory),
and to those who come to visit when doors
Let them in.

There is a table where I take my lunch:
cucumber sandwiches with cranberries and
a thermos of loose-leaf tea. I sit
watching the doors I can see, listening
to those I cannot.

Eventually, one opens. My first grade teacher
walks across the pine and brick floor
to take the stool opposite me. She whispers
her first name.

Doors open. Keystones shift deeper into their seats.

In the Unlocking Room my mother holds a quay.
Algae and barnacles drip between her fingers,
their watery strength collapsing under the weight of air.
Boats hang from her hair like marionettes;
she shakes her head and they swim past her face,
sails concealing her lips.

The Unlocking Room shrinks when I stay too long,
expands when I decide to leave, gathering the remnants
of my visit close.

I sweep the table clean
with the heel of my hand.
Unsure where to put the crumbs, I drop them
in my pockets.

When I go, I forget where they came from.

The Unlocking Room accordions closed,
so thin it can only be seen from one side,
one eye squinted, tongue pinched
between your teeth.

They grow between foundation stones

Rapunzel's hair was hyphae;
she lay down in moss & topsoil,
garter snakes circling her lips
tasting futures on the air.

Her hair grew & grew
meeting sycamore roots & birch
tracing footprints of ages
& fossils forgotten.

In the shade of a medieval folly
Rapunzel decided to wait
no more.

She buried herself in leaf litter
& wove her face a fungal
sleeping mask.

Ages after, princes came looking
for the maiden Gothel forgot.
But where a tower once stood
they found a faerie ring.

Pale mushrooms rising
kissing light instead of lips
sending their spores at last
to the ends of the world

carried on the boots
of oblivious knights.

conjuring mangroves

Everyone knows the witches
who grow by ages
in granite blocks exposed
to rough New England winters
still draped in thick
colonial smoke.

All have felt the embers
melting candy houses into
crystalline mass graves
watched over by listing
dispassionate historical markers.

Tell me: is your broomstick
really a palm frond?
Is your familiar
iguana-shaped?

Your All Hallow's Eve is
sticky with humidity,
frogs chirping under
a full moon.

Our graves hold bones,
yours: Spanish moss
trussed together
with tropical webs.

Your witches wear gauze
and sunscreen
while they fly over
haunted everglades.

From Connecticut to Key West
we send binding spells,
quarterly newsletters
remembering our sisters

whose graves have yet
to be marked.

Where We Felt
With Moss

At the table in the willow grove
all our feet are bare and damp.

A string connects our cuticles.
With each shared stroke, it hums

the music we share with the bees,
while mice shake chajchas

made from ladybug shells.
Our hands reach from one end

of the table—past milkweed seeds
and pewter beads the mourning doves

brought as gifts—to the other, where
we knit cocoons for wooly bears

and webs for lace weavers.
Where our fingers touch, needles grow.

We share them, left and right,
each project growing in the spaces

where our bodies make shade.
Clockwise we crochet jay nests,

sculpt exoskeletons and eggshells,
incise bark with memories.

Counterclockwise we felt coats
for butterflies and moths, tugging

tufts of moss from the ground
with our toes.

Everything dries in the dapples
between our crafts, tested for strength

by water striders. Under the light
of dusk we knot our strings together,

gnash our needles while
deer mice retreat.

As the moon rises our futures hatch
from teapots, clay halves rolling wet

into our laps.

Nobyl

Denali herds wild grass. She wraps strands around her
wrists up to her elbows
and walks from the edge of the sunrise
to the rim of the sunset, dragging the day
and the plains
behind her.

Fairhair breaks roads. His antlers crack
pavement into pebbles, disrupts
gravel and rolls it into earth. He walks
over lands that used to be called
streets, ensuring the people
have gone.

Basil paints with vines. His scurrying
dislodges paper scraps like dying
leaves as he climbs each crumbling building
and paints a landscape of the past, the future.
His murals color
high-rises into
hills.

Jamila spreads seeds like radiation,
millions of bombs dropped over roofs,
roads, memories. She beats her wings and
flaps
a breeze spun from her effort
to repopulate
Nobyl.

Santi carries the forest into the city.
His fur is dusted with pollen, his nose
driving sprouts through cracks. He follows the paths
drawn by all the Nobyl inhabitants, all the children
of disaster.

Qi guards the boundary.
Their roots hold the line, their branches
pull poison from the clouds.
They grow to cover the skeletons
that fumble and fall with the ages. They know
that Nobyl is the frontier, the first forest
to grow
from a city.

For a place in the family of things

i.
A dynasty divided by years of waves,
storms thundering, dragging,
cracking these shells away from
outside of myself. I was born
in seaweed, slick, wet, adrift.
I was born looking to anchor myself
in time, swirling
with the tide, riding out the storms
the winds tossed my way.

We are born waiting for the shore.

ii.
The place where family surges
and breaks and mends itself,
drawing the pieces together
like shadows coalescing before sunlight;
that is the place where the drifting stops.

Born seaweed, we seek this place and
we know it is a cove. In rockpools
and silhouettes of broken shells
with glacial memories I plant my life
in the crook of the past, extending a tendon
feeling into the world.

Primeval slime turns to blood and bile
and all the things decision is made of.

iii.
I reach this tidal rest
and among the bones of my mothers
I taste the salt of growing.

On the coast, all bets are collected. All lives cast free.

charybdis

see her:
dancing at the bottom
—whirlpool kisses—
streams of bubbles
i forgot to taste as i swam
gasping
in circles.

her toes are pointed fins
her hair the current
hugging me tighter
tighter, drawing me
down
to her show.

in the ocean's roar
she's laughing.
in the deepest darkness
her teeth shine
like abalone.

i'm sinking again
like yesterday and tomorrow
counting her fingers
her toes
her eyelashes batting the barnacles
away

she is smaller than i remember
happier than i was
more imperfect than i wanted
to see.

waves reflect tears
into laughter,
warp drowning
into dancing.

at the bottom she spins
and spins, spins
spins me in her skin,
enfolds me in a high tide of joy
washing the sand
from my eyes.

What do you remember about the earth?

It begins with sunset. So
maybe that is already
the future. It begins with
failure; trying comes after.
It began with a broken
twig, the crackle of death
under my foot. So
that's how we remember earth.
Beginnings aren't always first.
I began by falling—walking
came after. I picked myself
up in auburns and browns
and I cleared a path in
the wilderness but
there was always a footprint
before mine. There was always
another voice.

Maid Stone

"lie down on your stomach,
giving your breasts to the earth
and your back to me."

i lay down in the hills,
wrapping my arms around barrows &
burying my fingers in ancient calderas.

your legs straddled my hips,
gripping as you bent with a stone chisel
to cut into the chalk of me.

i dozed as you shaped me
awaking only when your hair brushed my shoulders
lips brushed my cheek.

"i'm finished," you said but didn't rise
didn't release me from the earth
pressing me deeper

we sank, your legs and me.
we sank into the hills until only my back
—your torso—breathed the day.

the horse you immortalized on me
shines and shines until the grass moves in
and you bend again at the waist

trimming back the world
to preserve your art.

While Alice sleeps in Wonderland

When Alice falls
I place a ribbon in my book
and walk through flowers
too wild for gardens.

When my sister dives
headfirst into another world
I take down my hair
and face the woods.

I don't have time—
an hour at most, before Alice returns
taking the door she opened
and shutting it again.

I leave the flowers behind
with my book and dear little Alice.
In the woods, I breathe again.
So little time.

I find your clearing and coat:
grey fur, red trim.
I follow your footprints
my breath short and wanting.

Your cottage shines even in daylight:
bright and open and smelling of sugar
and you.
Shedding your coat, I go inside.

Alice floats in a sea of her making
and I find you at your grandmother's oven.
We have so little time—Alice growing
big again, entangled in houses too small.

Our clothes cover the floor
and I count the minutes before
this world closes, before
the cards collapse.

Alice is playing croquet;
I am tangled in fingers and sheets
that smell of wolves.
Alice is angry. I am in love.

Before the court gathers
you kiss my left breast
and braid my hair, leaving me
so I won't see how you disappear.

Under the apple tree
I retrieve my book, face flushed,
heart curling to see you,
aching to lose you again.

When Alice climbs back into sleep
her head in the sunshine
I know you've gone—
your world closed, your cottage lost.

I no longer fit in holes in the ground
and mirrors are too shallow
for women
like us.

Alice, though.
Alice is quick. She is small.
Her dreams grow large enough
to carry ours

another day.

In the middle

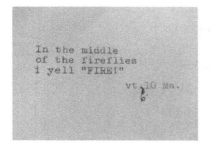

In the middle
of the fireflies
i yell "FIRE!"
                    vt 10 Ma.

In the middle of the fireflies
       the world is not diseased. Dande-
       lions sneeze seeds into the air like
       they don't care who gets sick, like
       sickness doesn't exist.

In the middle of the fireflies
       a ghost slides out of a horse-
       shoe. "Bring out your dead," she says
       to me. "Bring out your dead, but don't
       forget to breathe."

In the middle of the fireflies
>   sticks are burning. Smoke obscures
>   the stars and suddenly
>   space is not so far. All the stars
>   are here.

In the middle of the fireflies
>   I wear a mask of the brightest green.
>   My hands in glow-in-the-dark gloves
>   make animals in the night. Flap, roar,
>   canter like a rabbit into dawn.

In the middle of the fireflies
>   there is a plague in words, a mire
>   that absorbs grass and flattens
>   the hills the moles made. I sink,
>   my toes grabbing mud.

In the middle of the fireflies
>   they hold a bag for me. I reach
>   inside and fill my hands with flour.
>   I spin and spin and dust the summer
>   in caster sugar snow.

In the middle of the fireflies
>   fire flies, fire flies. Flies from my head
>   and catches the trees. The field burns and
>   mud cracks, cakes around my baking
>   feet. Smoke shades the morning.

In the middle
      I stand still.
      The sun reveals nothing I didn't already see
      in the light
      of the fire-
      flies.

Paper boats

"Can I tell you a secret?"

No. Let me tell one to you.

Under my skin it is midnight
moon shining full.
Between my eyes I planted a Perseid
and every midsummer it grows
three calendula blossoms.

Where my toes ought to be
I have ten regrets.
When I shave my legs
phoenixes crumble to ash
and bells melt into ice cubes.

My favorite color is you.
My favorite cake is
roses-painted-red.
My favorite dream is
being awake.

If you turn me around,
you can read my family tree
in the rivers of my pores.

Look at me straight on and I sound
like foghorns and mist.

At breakfast I like eating reflections.
For lunch – echoes.
For dinner I skip backwards
and kiss frogs into open pages.

Buy me something I'll love
and I'll sell it to the hills
to fund the digging
of graves.

Once a year, I bury everything
like the end of the Iron Age.

Tell me a secret and I'll tell you
something you've always known,
but been too frightened to ask.

Tell me a lie and I'll tell it back
in words that unmake
untruth.

Tell me – what do you want to see
hung up on the future?
What makes you so proud?

I have all my words.
Don't ask me to take on more.

That secret? Keep it.

There are rivers in your skin
and sirens in your hair.
Hold the words close because
thoughts float.

I've lost so many that way.
They're in your skin now,
in your singing hair.

What you decide to do with them
is a secret I'll never ask
to know.

At the wedding of Death and Time

We toast our futures and our pasts.
The marquee stands atop a barrow.
Sunlight warms our faces and We cry
for the possibilities We see reflected
in ice and candle wax.

She wears a gown of cobwebs, her face
veiled in moss. Flower girls drop
toadstools in her path—her bouquet
holds white lilies and nightshade.

He is robed in leaf litter, his hair
a crown of seeds.
His groomsmen pour wine
onto their feet.

The festivities last an age and a day
We watch the moon wax and wane,
their vows taken under a gibbous
they dance illuminated by a fading crescent.

No invitations were sent and none
received. All guests remembered
when the moss bloomed and seeds
cracked free of their shells—
the wedding was complete.

We shared a single pomegranate,
sweet and bitter soaking our tongues
as they departed into the dark
of a new moon.

At the funeral of Thought and Action

We raise our hands to the waning sun
clouds skip off their axes
and grass browns for want
of water.

They are laid at the base
of a crumbling well.
Her coffin is apple wood; his: glass.
Lilies cover them like promises.

When the hole has filled
We walk back to idling cars
our shadows one hour longer,
our lives reduced by same.

We ponder lingering
as the horizon lengthens,
turning retreating clouds
fever-red.

We depart in different directions
each holding a crumb
of the soil We left atop
their unquiet tomb.

At the birth of Song and Silence

We hold music too thin
for lyrics, our mouths working
in pantomime.

Clean towels hang from tender fingers
while collectively We hold
our breath.

The twins are born writhing
one loud, one mute
as the papers We clutch
to our thrumming hearts.

To each We give a birth chart
invoking the most distant stars.
To one: fire and Jupiter.
To one: water and Mars.

They are bathed in gin and chamomile,
their eyes wiped clean with dandelion fluff
and laid to sleep in a treble clef cot.

We watch over them under the shifting sky
humming all the names
we borrowed from the stars.

And windows for regrets

In the seams between bricks
too narrow for mortar
cracking into fragments

we planted a letter
to all our future selves.

You wrote in the foundations
to children we may never gain
of low tides & highways

burned bread & dry throats
hoarsely singing their way.

In bathroom tiles slick with soap scum
I wrote to every person
I'll never meet

all the stories I wish
to one day tell.

My words slid down
& circled the drain.

Between sheetrock & scaffolding
you folded all the hair you've lost.
Clipped nails, shed skin

baby teeth adrift
in past mistakes.

On the roof I planted us—
ivy, bugleweed, white violets
clustering around

disused chimneys
held together by moss.

We swore, once:
we'd never move from this—
our first & last house.

You wrapped yourself up
in the front walk

& I lay down in the arms
of the driveway.

We always knew:
beginning something means
ending something else.

While we lived, we forgot
how lovely it was to die.

Enshrouded in our enfeebled home
we keep the promises
others made on our behalf.

They may never read our remnants
but this house will live

—will die—
again.

Part Two: sirens

The Ossuary at
Ocean's End

We welcome you your bones
wrapped in seaweed and
ancestor's scales,
following the tides that led you
here
to us.

Lay them by tails
Lay them by shells that once
were not empty.
Lay them in waters too dark
to find a second
time.

We welcome your bones
too heavy to float
and make room
for a reef
of dead.

waves lap and salt
sinks
into arms
of all who once held,

continue holding—
even as oceans
end.

Iron, Glass, Slipper

On the mantle rest the ashes
of my grandmother,
arranged in her favorite pair
of iron shoes.
Winter nights I prop incense
smoking her spirit to rest.

On the kitchen counter my mother's
ashes fit perfectly
in her glass wedding pumps.
I position them to catch
morning sun turning tiles
rainbow & red.

By the front door my only
empty shoes wait
each day for me
to leave.

Red & sparkling, I know
they'll follow me from home
to places
like home,

Until I fill them forever
like the women who
dance & dance
their shoes
for ever
after.

Aequinoctium

behind my lungs she whispers
too deep.

In her echo my toes seek mycelium & darkness
holes widen to hold me
but moss recoils, knows
I am a stranger.

I promised to stop but I fight
ripping new wounds while my fractals form
underneath
she whispers
breathe once.

I gasp & gasp gasp gasp
clawing grass grasping
soil & rocks
hearing only her voice
my skin sprouts,
hardens where she planted me.

blink once.

Bark creeps across my eyes
stifles my voice while hers grows
a whisper to a gale.

Ax & spade are last to vanish,
consumed under my shroud
of withered leaves.

Killing whale

caught under   the waves
        of the glorious   purple
night
        thump   thump

rippling all   over   and   around
                         into
        herself.

her
        song of orcas
herds soft
scrapes savage—

        skin scaled, eyes wide
            black & white

playing in the darkened   abyss

          beat   beat
thump

                          even darkness has
a   heart.
                    Even darkness has

lips.

Victor II

I made you.
I made you, and I'm sorry.

Without the first tie, the whole scaffold of flesh
and sail comes tumbling
away.
there's nothing but a mass of crumpled
skin, sopping wet.

it moves away, searching for some sort of
delivery, some stitch to make it
whole.
Or maybe what it wants is undoing,
an agent to come unbind it from you,
from itself.

There is one out there who can peel apart crescendos
like layers on an onion,
sift through the melting mass
and drag organ after organ away,
dropping them together in a jar
to knock about,

hollow in isolation.

Maybe this is what it wants, after how you failed.
Maybe this is how you should repay it.

You step forward,
waiting for it to ooze away,
out of sight and out of mind.

You have all the power to run.
But instead you stand and watch
that thing you tried and failed
to create
sag
and die.

I made you of myself.
I should have recognized my mistake.

your toes edging to the place where the porch dips
away, sloping down to the mud,
and the thing.

>   tendrils of its half-formed body
>   spread
>   reaching,

the trees tremble
yet their branches hold on to the stars.
They remain.

>   *I wanted you gone*
>   *as much as I wanted*
>   *you.*

>   You step off the porch.

mud seizes you, whispering
all the words of all the languages
you refused to learn.

>   reclaiming flesh and sailcloth
>   from which you began,

skin mixes with clay, too late
for either now.

Birth is another type of murder.
Never clean
never quick.

What made you
think
you could
leave?

death shadow

my breath surrendered
my heart relinquished
my pulse laid down
to blet.

it is a glorious thing,
losing everything.

in stopping I feel
less and more and outside
skin that never fit—
first too tight,
then loose & loose
and lost.

I let go of it all &
it wasn't my choice.
this is the best, I think.
lying blameless,
lying bare.

I watch myself bloat,
purge fluids and solids
& spirits borrowed
from my mother,
grandmothers stacked
through millennia
of dying.

this is my favorite bed—
when at last they find me,
peel me up and fold me
through a door I never locked,
a shadow remains.

millefleurs darkened by my gravity,
a pattern I hope they never wash
away.

I am sleeping here still
sinking deeper
wrapping my ending
in flannel sheets
sorted by my mother
pressed by my grandmother
wrought by wrinkled fingers
over ages & ages
to hold me last
and no one
else.

Take me as prescribed

I folded myself into a pill
contorted my shoulders and
hunched my knees,
flattened my face to match
the shell I urge you to swallow.

Inside it is milky blue,
whorls of morphine
fireworking like blackness
under my dreaming lids.

My feet lose feeling
waiting to be consumed.
My hair senesces
and I am bald as your teeth.

Please choose quickly.
Drink water or absinthe,
orange juice or Kool-Aid
laced with past mistakes.

I am the one lying
at the bottle's bottom
colored orange by the kitchen light.
You can't miss me – I'm last.

Drink. Swallow.
Press your tongue
to the roof of your mouth and soon
I'll be with you

always.

Topsoil

When I lost my skin
I found petals
work just as well.

Folding dahlias into daffodils
tulips between jasmine,
hosta on my feet &
bleeding hearts around my throat.

Where some skin escaped you
I planted moss in pores:
cultivated fiddleheads in place
of follicles
& watered the creases
you forgot.

When you uprooted my face,
laid bare muscles bleeding
like grapevines cut too short—

I seeded the wounds with thyme
myrtle, aster, yarrow & heather.
My back now thrives
in lavender and phlox.
My heart shelters under daisies
hugging hyacinths close.

Colors run
like tears
like defiance
like survival.

This isn't your garden.
You may have my skin
but I am something
stronger.

I grow more each day
blooming, filling the space
you used to burn
with shade.

And it dries and dries

In my mind a butterfly catches pneumonia:
Flap flap the world is changed.

There's a second life but not a first,
there's you and no there's just me—
no we no us just just just
iron and
lilies and
coffin nails.

All I want to see is darkness today,
tomorrow.

But the light keeps intruding
even after the candle, snuffed by heaving breaths,
snuffed enough to undo the whole legacy of definitions
I've been trying to land on, trying to find
in darkness and heat.

Did you know oil has eyes?
They watch when we drill through lungs
through heart, searching
arching
aching in the earth.

Earth full of bones and mucus.

They said: find a world that never ends,
a globe that never circumferences,
a planet without time outside of time
inside a box under a table
with three legs.

Listen to the drill
deeper, into a hollowed-out sphere
crafted of papier mâché
but using too much glue
like we always did.

There's nothing left
(but lots left, covering the whole vast
world)
an embarrassing mess that no
one
wants to clean
up.

So I bend down
and tear off a page
to write on: ending lines from every corner of a circle.

Tomorrow and tomorrow and tomorrow
faltering, wheezing, dripping
over the edge, pooling off the pages
because the glue is still wet,
still sticking and dragging away my words,
pouring over my feet.

Stop. Step.
Step two.

there should have been a step one, but there isn't.
It was swallowed, see, no—hear—*here*,
in the smallest hole you find
among trembling butterfly bodies:
twitch twitch
itch, a scrapped memory hovering
at the back of your eyelids,
just out of reach.

Step, step, step.

Mothers become stepmothers in fairy tales

In daguerreotypes they conceal us
under quilts, screened in scratched-out
ink, hiding on the left on the
right side of our children.
We are born in birthing
our new ghost lives.

Mothers cannot be bad mothers.
Mothers cannot be good mothers.
Women cannot un-mother
de-mother, never-mother, self-
save through emptying
being empty
facing empty
dying empty.

We are born to mother
mother mother smother
our lives in the dreams
of others whose being
Unmade ours.

In fairy tales there are
no mothers anymore.
We fall back into the past
off-screen, under screens
hidden in the artificial shadows
of our children.

Stay still
so the camera can
cut you out.

This stepping of us,
titles be-stepped, ties
Unmothered, severed
deleted detached despised
in adding just one
word.

Step.
Step.
Step

on her and see
her melt away

leaving her children
alone again alone
standing, staring into the lens
she cannot
see.

For this meal we thank her

The Willow Wolf has asked
"What do you see in me?"

Each night we meet
beneath a moon that wanes
and waxes unseen. Tinted
clouds describe her face;
I shiver under wraps,
brocade the night
embodied.

When I visit the Willow Wolf
I bring a basket of cheese
and Meat.
We dine together under
hidden stars, trees
whispering too loud.

I tried to stay away from her,
from this place adorned in rot—
leaf decay and owl pellets
webs of fungi like
summer snow.

I cannot stay away from her
even after all she's done.
Her teeth are long and lovely
Her ears so soft, so warm
Her eyes draw and draw me
into darkness again,
again.

Tonight when she asks me
why I sit why I lie with her
in a tangle of claws
and skin

I tear a cut of Meat in half,
share shadows too bright
—too warm.

"You're all I have," I say
I mean it—as I mean everything
Every act.

She smiles at me
and we lounge together
consuming the last halves
of grandmother's
flesh.

correspondence

i wrote a letter to death today.
i signed my name, and all.

i asked him how to cope
with feeling so alone.

thought maybe he would know,
what with the business he runs

so smoothly, after all—
he's been at it quite a while.

i suppose it was silly to wish
for some kind of response.

i'm sure he's very busy
reaping *earth to earth*

but i thought maybe we had something
after all these years.

he's met my parents
and my cousin too.

        he had a run in with my niece
        and a cat or two.

i thought that surely by now,
he'd heard about me.

but it's been four weeks,
and no answer's come in the mail.

i don't know what to do.

this big house is so empty
(now the cats have gone, too).

     maybe

i'll write another
—*ashes to ashes*—

or maybe i'll wait
and ask him what he thinks

dust to dust,
face
     to
          face.

Mary Celeste

Swell below my intestines,
break, regroup, rise again.

gurgling hunger rends the night;
desperate hunger shakes the sky

up, down, tossed this way by
fate, tossed that way by

a misplaced heartbeat, a misjudged
destination. Intestine swell,

stomach turn, belly of the beast:
the temper-tossed waves.

Calm me, tell the sea:
recalculate the stars, recalibrate

the senses. Misjudged, ill-placed
faith, in these treacherous waters

from shore to endless horizon,
falling off the edge of the world

shrinking into the distance,
convulsing, converging. We took

this path in error, we took
an empty ship into

overflowing sensation. Creaking
timber, swelling sails, lifeboat

splashes, plunges us
together into history.

Squeezing hands, thrashing
dreams; bear west

onward to the unknown, swells
stretching and imploding into

water drops on
chapped skin.

Oddkin

on the grey liminals
of the ocean—shorelines—
places of salvage
where spirits idle &
futures
wonder
wander
under the captive witness
of a disheveled sky

multiplicity unfurls in seashells,
mussels cracking open
tasting the danger on the
shape-shifting breeze.

I found
a piece of broken sapphire
smoothed by the tantrums of the sea.

cylinders collapse when waves wash
through them; we find their
bones wrapped in the dust
of ancestors forgotten.

my pockets, distended with exiles,
carry broken migrants from
worlds connected by dead things—

behind me the bridge widens
reflecting a screaming sky.

and

Then I will dig my fingers into the clay
searching for maybe, for what,
caked joints with ash in the gaps
where questions once hung. Then
I will shed the pebbles & make way
for gravel to line my seams,
struck from what I was, patched,
glaring in the sun. Then I will
carve into myself the words
I forgot to speak, so when I sit
cross-legged in the field

my voice is legible

for ages into now.
Then all that I wrought or ripped out
of the soil of my beginning, falling back,
collapses with the dawn
And I am nothing more
than what rude armament was made
of me

when it all began.

Huios: Phaeton's Flight

that morning, my father lit a candle for me
to guide my ride over sea and shore.
I threw myself open, rising, ready.

thermals buoyed me, pulling
me ever on, yet always keeping
me at a distance, keeping me
just far enough away.

I rose and rose until I was sailing
through a cloudbank of smoke
and flame.

my eyes filled with fire, and I remembered my name to him.

son. sun.

step one, two—
two hearts, side by side.
step one, two—
higher than before.

step one into the sky,
step two into me.
step out of me.

we opened our eyes and saw dawn
falling with stars around his ribcage,
opening wide onto eight hooves
straining free of our bony stable
riding high on the horizon.

our charge led him on out of himself
into the mist.
into the fall.
nostrils flared against the flame,
our legs kicking the air.

taut skin, stained sunrise-red.

I took down the tendons of life
and wove them into ropes to hold my fears,
ropes to hold my ambitions.

in the pre-dawn light I fastened them
to part of myself
wrapping them round and round my life,
cinching tight.

in the pre-dawn light we held tight
flying into the mist
into the smoke
into the future.

we flew in captivity
bound by ropes of his fashioning;
bound and bloody and scorched by desire.

we rose over whole, unbroken skin.
the higher we got, the rounder it became:
speckled and spangled
imperfect, bruised.

in the distance: twirling stem
straining into the atmosphere.
sometimes red, sometimes green,
with a broad white sea where his teeth sunk in—
tearing flesh and exposing core.

seeds falling out of the world
into empty shadow.

when the muscles in my arms lost their tension
reins slipped out of my hands.
snapping skin, snapping sails—
torn, shredded by light.

useless wheels skipped off their axles
forging their own path through the mist
and dissolving back into the past
until all that touched the ground were fallen leaves

red and yellow and orange like the chariot.

gold, gilt, blood.

I reached the apex,
staring down at all the things I hadn't made
all the things that weren't mine to create
but mine to shine upon.

when the time was right, I dove
and snatched the apple from the ether
biting in, spraying ocean to the stars.

as we were falling, we recalled his name to him.

son. sun.

Heel to Toe

My grandmother put silver
slippers on my feet; she told
me to walk in them, click
my heels.

Her slippers glittered like stars as
I teetered from bed to wall
click click click

Back with her at bed's end
I stepped out and found blood lining
dried brown spots adorning
the heel of one, toe of the other.

I asked her how she cut
her feet inside shoes that always
always fit her perfectly.

She said nothing, said to put
her lovely slippers
on again.

My feet grew to fit—
cover the stains and click
my way to work
—click me home
again.

My grandmother died
when I was twenty-five
lying alone in that bed, gray hair
a veil across her face.

I found her amidst tangled
quilts, unscarred feet
bare

like mine used
to be.

The Art of Betraying Others for Food

First, one must be selective.
Very few dishes can be valued above
the lives of your loved ones,
or the world.

Case: Items labeled for consumption
Arranged on a glass end table, they plead.
Drink me, Eat me. Honor this request.
Pick your potion, select your quantity. Destroy
private property in anticipation of another
Bite.

Case: Bread crumbs
To rid oneself of meddlesome
stepchildren, charge a Dustbuster
to its full potential. Follow the trail they made,
cleaning all the way.
These crumbs are perfect
for stuffing.

Case: Candy house
>   Set your oven to 400 degrees.
>   Wrap your witch in aluminum
>   to prevent dry meat.
>   Roast, toast, and finish
>   with candied walls.

Case: A basket of goodies
>   Here is a crossroads.
>   Your tongue lolls. For sweets,
>   murder one girl. But if you are
>   the girl?

Case: Wolf meat
>   Take one knife and sharpen it
>   next to a cottage and an ax.
>   Skin, mindful not to stain
>   grandmother's best linens.

Case: Sons who rape
>   One meat pie, seasoned
> and served as an appetizer
> for blood.

>   The aperitif is always

Delicious.

the glaciers made
her deep

When I was born, the Valley whispered into my ear:
"These hills will hold you. These hills
will keep you safe."

I listened and I walked the paths she laid
across her chest, following the murmur
of the river at her heart.

Each time I looked up from her soul
I saw them—holding the Horizon
at bay.

Trees formed a lattice to dapple the sun;
at night they played tricks with the moon.
She sleeps on, swaddled in promises.

Awake, I have seen what waits beyond the Valley.
I do not tell her, though it comes closer
every year.

I do not interrupt her dreaming pulse
as the Horizon leans over her hills,
breathing ripples onto calm water.

saving daylight

I lost an hour this morning—
let it slip between the sheets
caught up in dead skin
& exhaustion trickling under
lucent dreams unseen.

I lost my way in March
when spring yielded the front
to winter, gales rolling unfaced
over tulips just struggling
to bloom.

In snowmelt I lost my being
shimmering blinding in the waxing sun.
I tried to drink myself back,
swallowing icicles like swords
until all my bones were frozen.

Between dead branches I thought
there could be no losing,
no fraying of time and purpose—
but I was wrong, hiking into dapples
where soon my footprints crunched away.

I thought we could save daylight:
make her pure, cancer-free.
I thought we could shave away her
climate-altering tendency
like stubble & ingrown green.

This morning I gave her one hour
of my future, always dwindling.
She took it kindly, offered me warmth
& cold beyond the season.
I know

no matter what I give her
she can't help her growing,
tingling to burning, my hands seized
on the bellows of her beckoning.
she tells me:

next
       year
make
       it
two.

Wait when ice forms
over my fingertips

like acrylic nails,
biting through skin and overwhelming
my eyes

my heart isn't strong—it never was—
and I saw the novae exploding across
your face and I wanted their fire

I dreamt of stardust and murder;
your lips like a coffin seal out the
enemy of life and they
stop and never stop
but I want to see them start

oh just once let me start
let me talk when I know I can't
and I know my teeth are shifting
and my gums bleed every night

but it's okay because you're permeable
and we can feel together and
you bleed beneath me and I scream

yes because we did it and it hurt
but scars tell us where we were
and I was and
you were too.

I wear my scars with pride
because getting this far—
it hurts.

Syph

lichen creeping up my edges
my skin a moldering
doorframe, a portal
disused, wetness the creak
of absent maintenance.

My lungs thickly varnished,
sticky under bare feet stepping through
breaths
drifting no-smoke current
but nicotine left its mark already
an artist in shades of
bronze

I am the stale scent of a place inhabited
by incidental movement

and my capillaries taste
like fire and filament
weighed by toxicity,
a tangled miasma
of breaths traded
wants for wants, admonitions
commands
surrender.

Behind a door a scene is carried out
in shuffling
and we fly through, buoyed
on the wings of our sexual
transgression onto

a threadbare rug
stained
with our soot.

Coronation

because a crown
        has spikes. its shape inherited
from the debt we never paid
to the stars.

because a star is crowned
        by fire.
        oblivion in place of purple
        velvet and ermine.

crown of thorns
of flames
so heavy with precious things
        it breaks the bearer's neck.

crowns have ever sought to weaken.
       Because a coronation is really
       an execution.
out with the old. in with the Always Has Been.
A chain of heredity.
A chain of tradition.
a band of silver.
a chain.

In gold the crowned ascends,
       descends,
sits at the bottom of a family tree.
The only way to rise: death.

Corona of stars, corona unchanging.
       corona enduring.

necks break and

spires rise. the every king

       is nothing
but
       a hatstand,

a pillar of flesh
to support
the ever

crown.

Seeing-holes

He removes his mask last,
hips swaying pendulous
stage lights blinding
white his perfect body
sweatless, weightless.

His burlesque ends in broken china
the shards of his face quivering
swaying with his dance
while silent watchers wave
in place of applause.

the front row feels Him,
his gaze rippling our edges
recalling the breaths we left
outside his curtained hall.

He dances naked, as naked
as we could hope
were we anything more
than reflections in trembling porcelain.

tonight His performance captures,
holds us in our interim.
it is as special as the one before
and what comes next.

folding his bones back, He retreats
behind the diaphanous waves
that divide his death
from ours.

alone *en masse,* we are here
still watching the shaking pieces
of the ruby mask He wore.

between this dance and the next
shadows shuffle and
He returns to an audience
strikingly different,
strikingly the same.

He enchants our leftover thoughts
to stray from the rooms we wonder
exist beyond, behind.

His burlesque enfolds,
intrudes
entices us to stay
to watch him
again.

vigil

i have left the grass behind
filled with ajuga, violets,
hyacinths you love
phlox in purple and white.

between your buzzing i want to tell you
i cannot leave entirely.
i am stuck in yellow and black
bars prickling with summer.

there is no one left to wander
between your wingbeats
to whisper my news
to you.

last of my kind, i come to you
swirls of pollen remain—
last of hair, skin, entrails
run out of fortunes.

no one came to tell you of our ending.
no one remembered
we created laws
to preserve our dying.

dust on autumn breeze
i hope you hear me,
words soaked in honey
over your busy melody.

We have finished.
We have ended.
We have no more wings
to beat in the sun.

no voices now remain
to name the forgotten.

with my fading, I breathe
our final song
to you who sing
under hidden gardens of gold:

goodbye, goodbye.
i will miss us.

ACKNOWLEDGEMENTS

There are too many people to thank, too many hands that—to greater and lesser extents—helped steer me to this place.

From my earliest to latest influences, I'd like to express gratitude to Emily Dickinson, Elizabeth Bishop, Ocean Vuong, Danez Smith, Katherine Larson, Theodora Goss, Anna Maria Hong, and all the other poets whose work drives me to make mine better.

Thank you to my incredible mentors: Robert V.S. Redick, David Anthony Durham, and JJ Amaworo Wilson, in the Stonecoast MFA Program. Especial gratitude to my cohort, and the Coven that has stayed with me, reading drafts and offering support through all struggles. Words are magic.

I must thank my stellar agent, Amy Collins, and J.D. Harlock for editing this collection. Huge thanks to Justine Norton-Kerston for believing in my work and making this collection a reality.

To every magazine and anthology that published poems reprinted in this collection: thank you for your passionate promotion and editorial touches. Thank you also to the friends I found online and at conferences—you make this community a wonderful place to be.

Thank you to my family for not stopping me when I switched my major from biology to English. You believed I would make it more than I did.

Finally, thank *you* for holding this book—digitally or physically—in your hands. I hope these little worlds found a shared language with yours.

About the Author

Marisca Pichette wrote her first story using quill and ink, sitting on a rock in the Western Massachusetts woods, a leatherbound journal balanced on her knees. Since then, she has published stories and poems across genres, with work appearing in *Strange Horizons, The Magazine of Fantasy & Science Fiction, Fireside Magazine, Flash Fiction Online, Vastarien: A Literary Journal, PseudoPod,* and *PodCastle,* among many others. She makes her home next to the woods that continue to influence her, busily filling the pages of a new journal.

CAGED OCEAN DUB
Glints & Stories

DARE SEGUN FALOWO

Coming June 20, 2023

Pre-Order at
www.android-press.com/bookstore

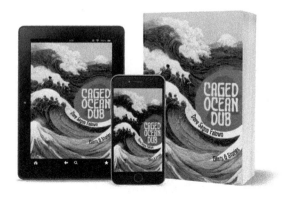

Android Press
Science Fiction & Fantasy Punks
www.android-press.com

CPSIA information can be obtained
at www.ICGtesting.com
Printed in the USA
BVHW050738080323
659912BV00008B/50

9 781958 121146